EVERYBODY SING GLORY!

A PRAISE and WORSHIP YOUTH Musical for CHRISTMAS

Created by Luke Gambill and Johnathan Crumpton

Arranged by Luke Gambill

Worship Leader Narration by Jonathan Lee

AVAILABLE PRODUCTS:

Choral Book	45757-2595-7
CD Preview Pak	45757-2595-1
Listening CD	45757-2595-2
Split-Track Accompaniment CD	45757-2595-3
Praise Band Audio Stem Files	45757-2595-4
Split-Track Accompaniment DVD (with .Mov Files on Disc 2)	45757-2595-6
Rhythm/Chord Charts	45757-2595-9
Soprano Rehearsal Track CD	45757-2596-0
Alto Rehearsal Track CD	45757-2596-5
Tenor Rehearsal Track CD	45757-2596-6
Bass Rehearsal Track CD	45757-2596-7
Drums Rehearsal Track CD (Drums-Left, Full Mix-Right)	45757-2596-1
Bass Guitar Rehearsal Track CD (Bass Guitar-Left, Full Mix-Right)	45757-2596-2
Guitar Rehearsal Track CD (Acoustic-Left, Electric-Right)	45757-2596-3
Piano/Keyboard Rehearsal Track CD (Piano-Left, Full Mix-Right)	45757-2596-4

www.brentwoodbenson.com

a division of

© MMXIV Brentwood-Benson Music Publications, 101 Winners Circle, Brentwood, TN 37027.
All Rights Reserved. Unauthorized Duplication Prohibited.

CONTENTS

Love Will Save the World 3

Newborn King 21

O Come, O Come, Emmanuel 29

Sing 39

O Rejoice 50
    with O Holy Night!

King of Heaven 59

Holy, Holy, Holy (God with Us) 68

Gospel of Love 81
    with Hark! the Herald Angels Sing

Love Will Save the World

Words and Music by
DAVID MOFFITT, CARL CARTEE
and JONATHAN LEE
Arranged by Luke Gambill

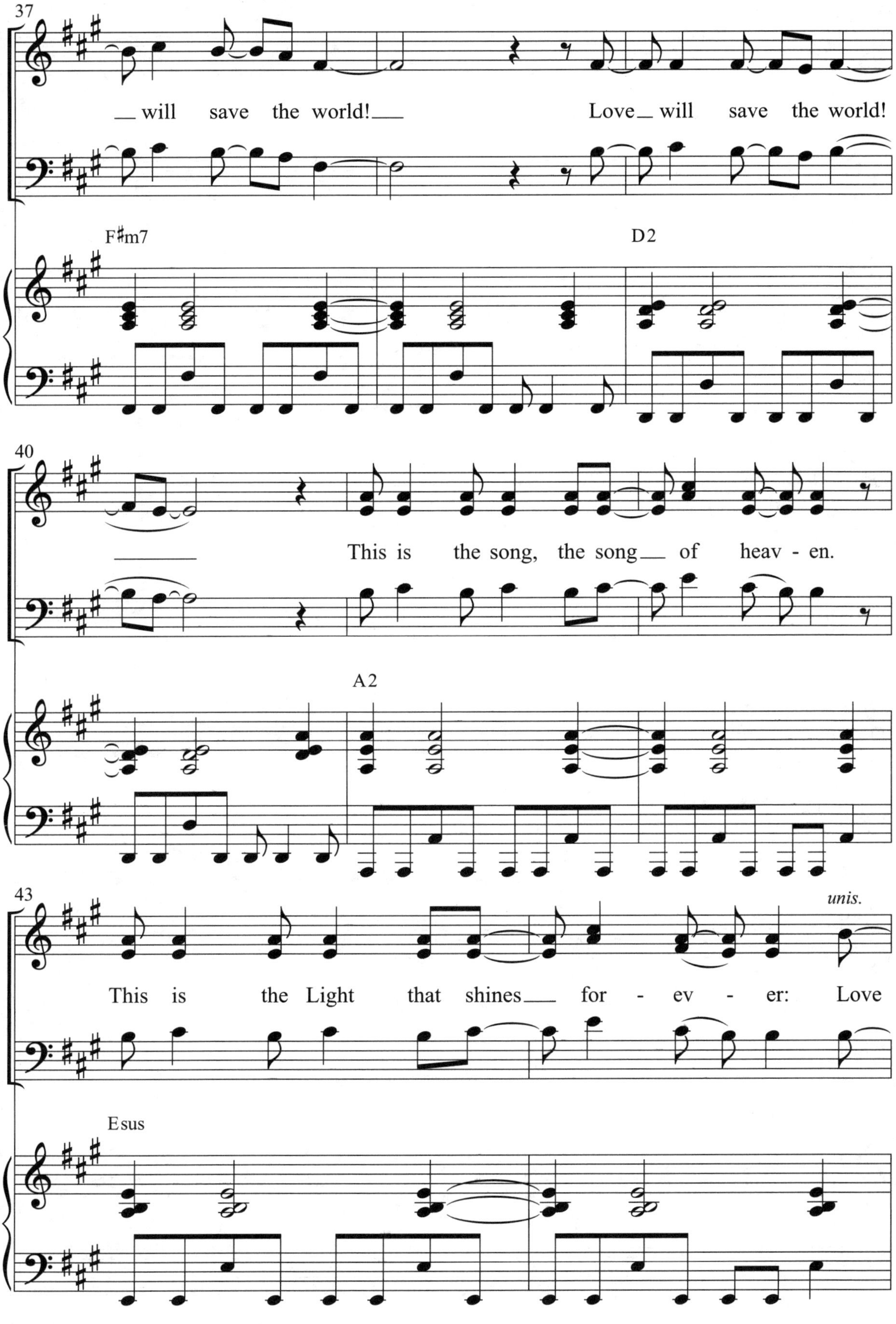
37
will save the world!
Love will save the world!
F♯m7
D2
40
This is the song, the song of heav - en.
A2
43
unis.
This is the Light that shines for - ev - er: Love
Esus

Newborn King

Words and Music by
JEFF PARDO and BRYAN BROWN
Arranged by Luke Gambill

NARRATOR: Hallelujah! Glory to our God! The Light of the world has come. *(Music starts)* He has come to bring hope. He has come to bring life. Now let us sing together, for our newborn King has come.

© Copyright 2014 worshiptogether.com Songs / Meaux Hits / Bears in the Bowl
(Administered at CapitolCMGPublishing.com). All rights reserved. Used by permission.
PLEASE NOTE: Copying of this music is NOT covered by the CCLI license. For CCLI information call 1-800-234-2446

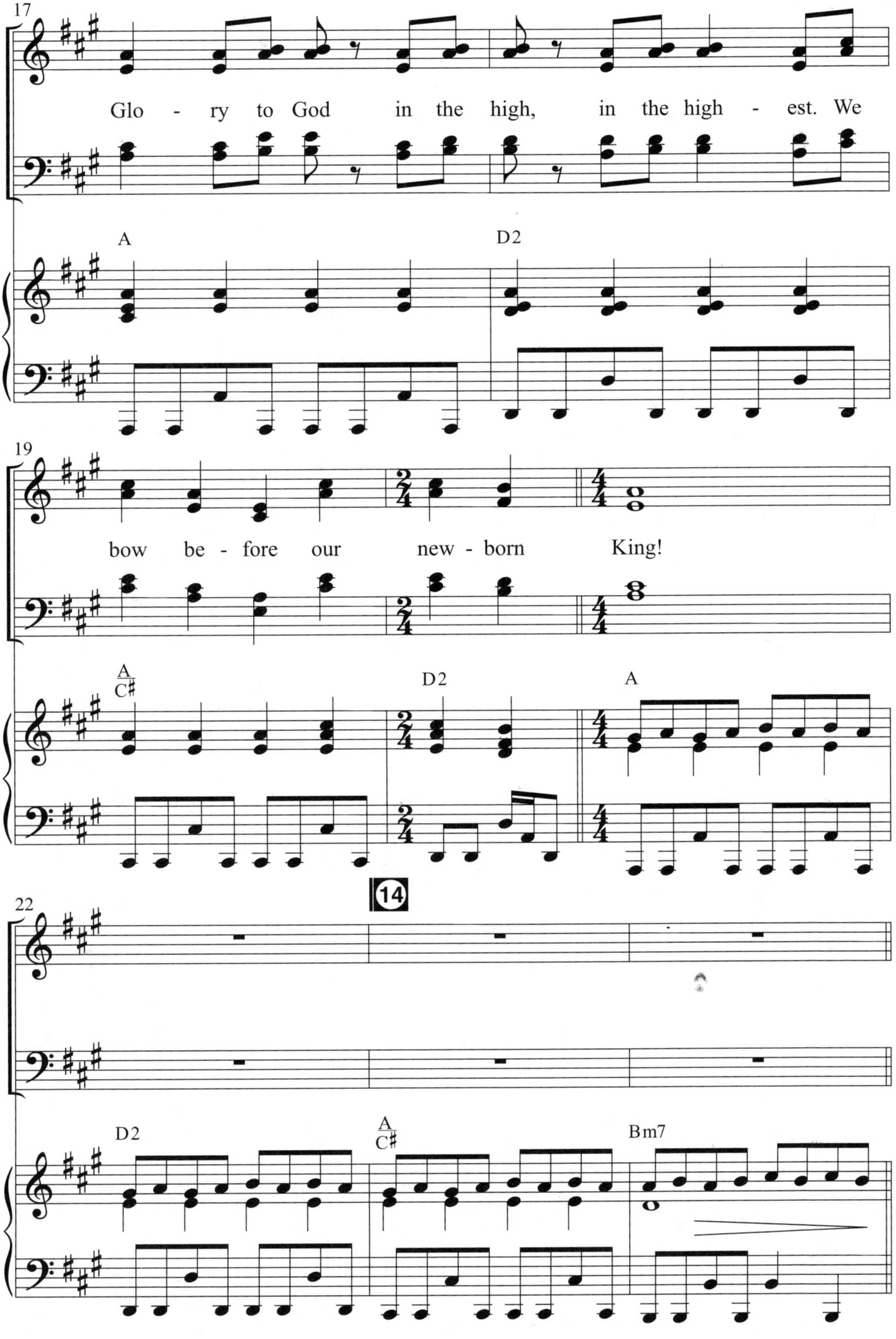
17
Glo - ry to God in the high, in the high - est. We
A
D2
19
bow be - fore our new - born King!
A
C♯
D2
A
22
14
D2
A
C♯
Bm7

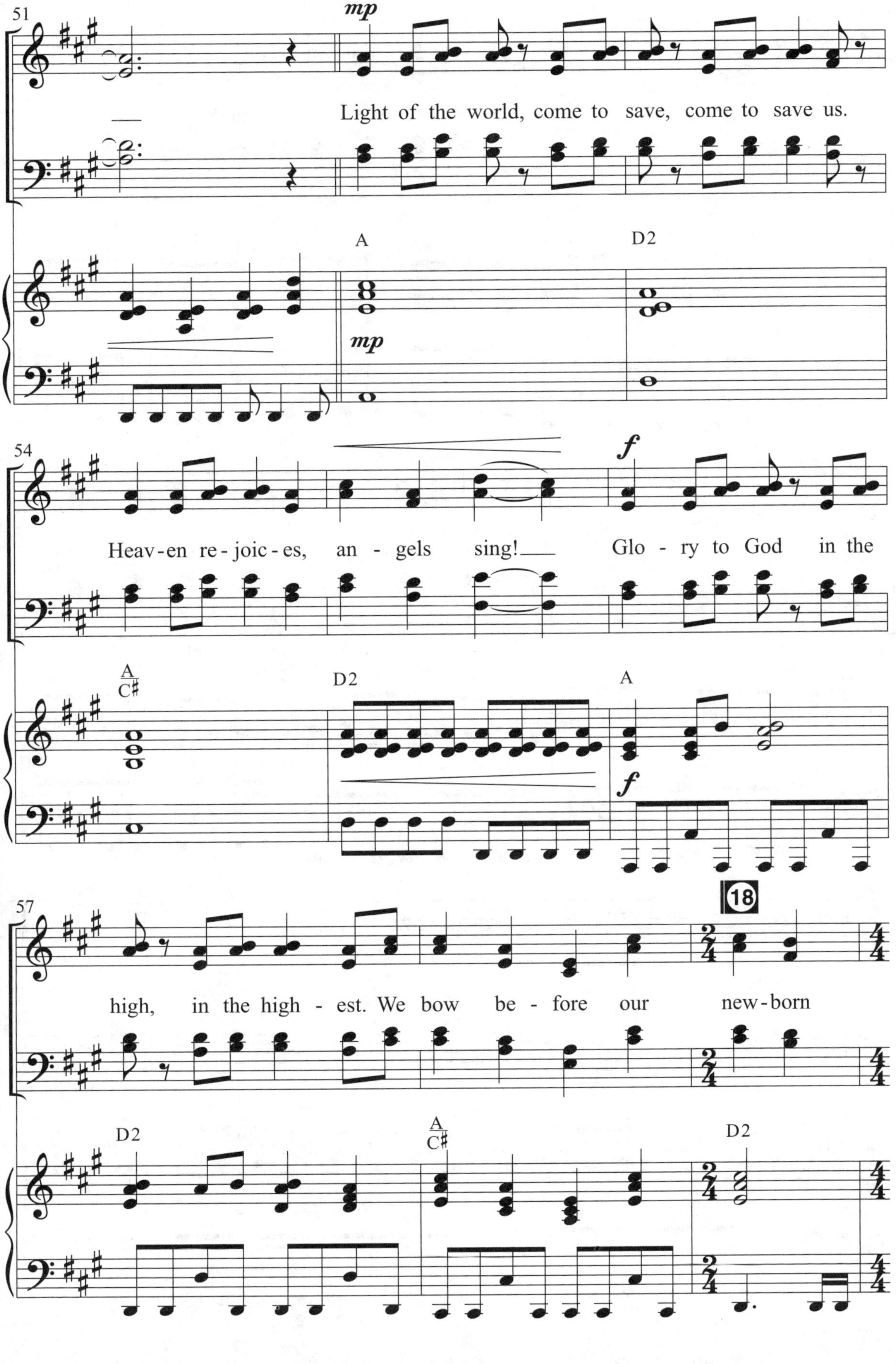
51
mp
Light of the world, come to save, come to save us.
A
D2
mp
54
f
Heav-en re-joic-es, an - gels sing! Glo - ry to God in the
A/C♯
D2
A
f
57
18
high, in the high - est. We bow be - fore our new-born
D2
A/C♯
D2

O Come, O Come, Emmanuel

Traditional Latin Hymn
New Music and Lyrics by
DAVID CROWDER, JACK PARKER,
JEREMY BUSH, MARK WALDROP,
MIKE DODSON and MIKE HOGAN
Arranged by Luke Gambill

NARRATOR: It was written: for to us a child is born, to us a son is given, and the government will be on His shoulders. *(Music starts)* And He will be called Wonderful Counselor, Mighty God, Everlasting Father, Prince of Peace! Oh, how we have longed and waited for that day, the day that we would be delivered. And now that day has come. Emmanuel, our God with Us, has come to set us free.

© Copyright 2011 worshiptogether.com Songs / sixsteps Music / Inot Music / Wacotron 3000 / Hoganmike Music (ASCAP)
(Administered at CapitolCMGPublishing.com). All rights reserved. Used by permission.
PLEASE NOTE: Copying of this music is NOT covered by the CCLI license. For CCLI information call 1-800-234-2446.

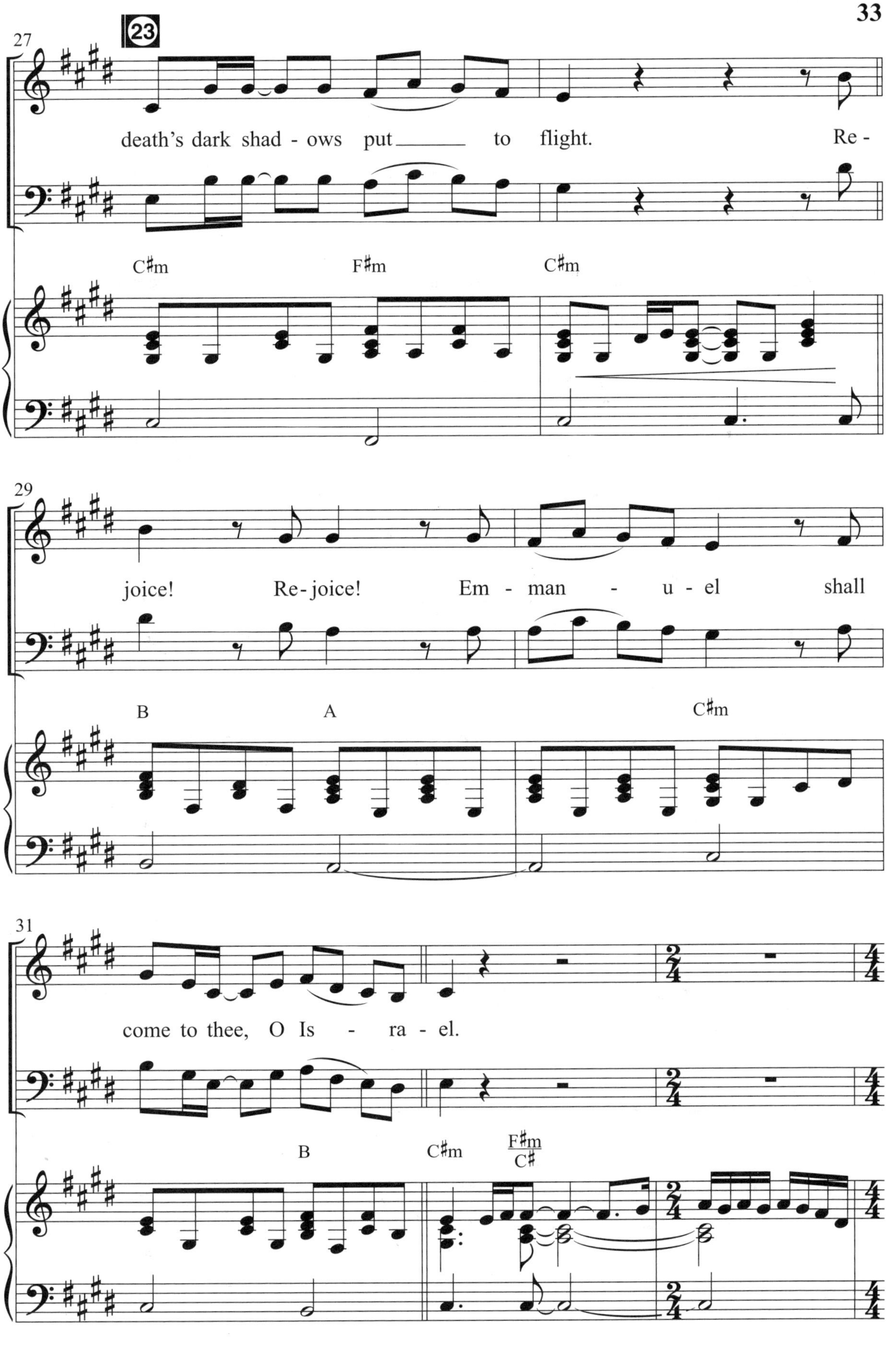
23
27
death's dark shad - ows put to flight. Re -
C♯m F♯m C♯m
29
joice! Re-joice! Em - man - u - el shall
B A C♯m
31
come to thee, O Is - ra - el.
B C♯m F♯m/C♯

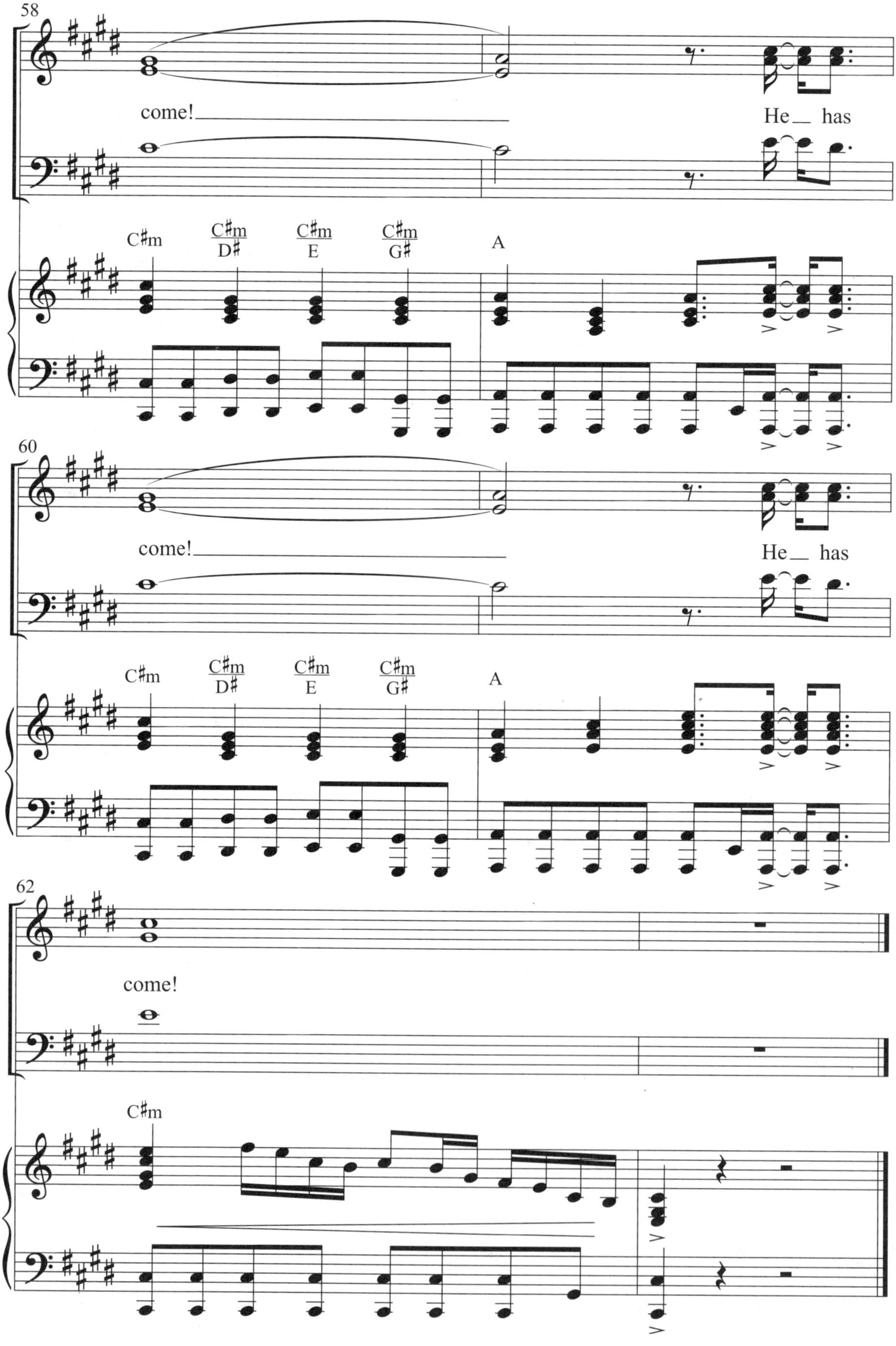
58
come!
He has
C♯m
C♯m/D♯
C♯m/E
C♯m/G♯
A
60
come!
He has
C♯m
C♯m/D♯
C♯m/E
C♯m/G♯
A
62
come!
C♯m

Sing

**Words and Music by
JOSH WILSON and JEFF PARDO
Arranged by Luke Gambill**

NARRATOR: *(Music starts)* Let us lift our voices and shout it out. For it is only by His grace that we are saved! We were lost, but now we are found! So, everybody let's come together and sing, "Glory to God in the highest." Come on, let's sing it out!

Ev-'ry bit of his-to-ry,____ and ev-'ry sin-gle breath we breathe has

© Copyright 2008 Meaux Hits (ASCAP) (Administered at CapitolCMGPublishing.com) / Simple Tense Songs
(Administered by Simpleville Publishing, LLC). All rights reserved. Used by permission.
PLEASE NOTE: Copying of this music is NOT covered by the CCLI license. For CCLI information call 1-800-234-2446.

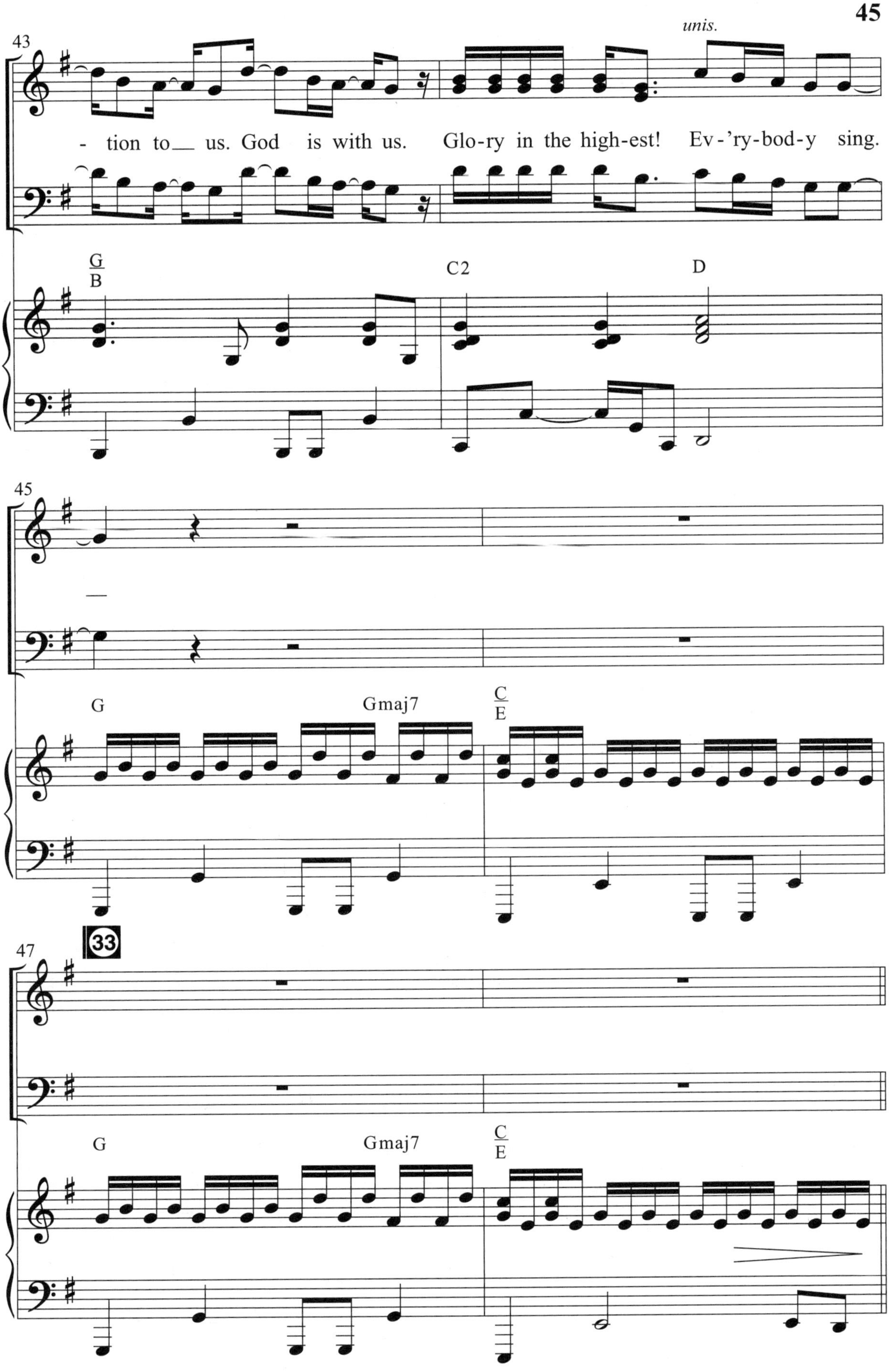
43
unis.
- tion to __ us. God is with us. Glo-ry in the high-est! Ev-'ry-bod-y sing.
G/B
C2
D
45
G
Gmaj7
C/E
47
33
G
Gmaj7
C/E

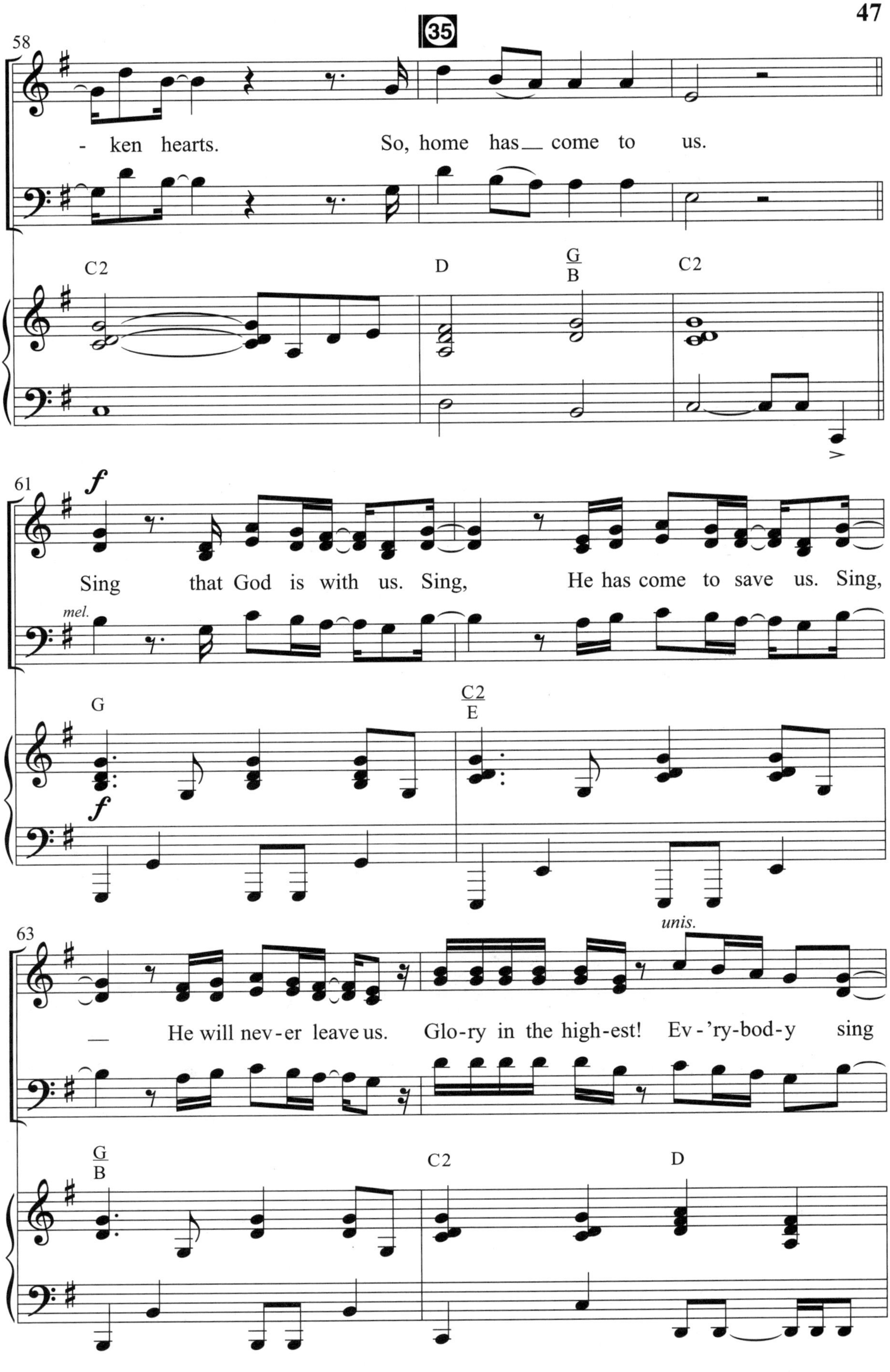

58
35
- ken hearts. So, home has come to us.
C2
D
G/B
C2
61
f
Sing that God is with us. Sing, He has come to save us. Sing,
mel.
G
C2/E
f
63
He will nev-er leave us. Glo-ry in the high-est! Ev-'ry-bod-y sing
unis.
G/B
C2
D

O Rejoice
with O Holy Night!

Words and Music by
MIA FIELDES
Arranged by Luke Gambill

NARRATOR: In the beginning was the Word and the Word was with God and the Word was God. *(Music starts)* Then the Word became flesh and dwelled among us. He came to make a way to bring light into our darkness — Heaven's Child sent down to deliver us. So, now let us rejoice and sing it out that our Lord has come.

© Copyright 2005 Hillsong Music Publishing (APRA)
(Administered in the U.S. and Canada at CapitolCMGPublishing.com). All rights reserved. Used by permission.
PLEASE NOTE: Copying of this music is NOT covered by the CCLI license. For CCLI information call 1-800-234-2446.

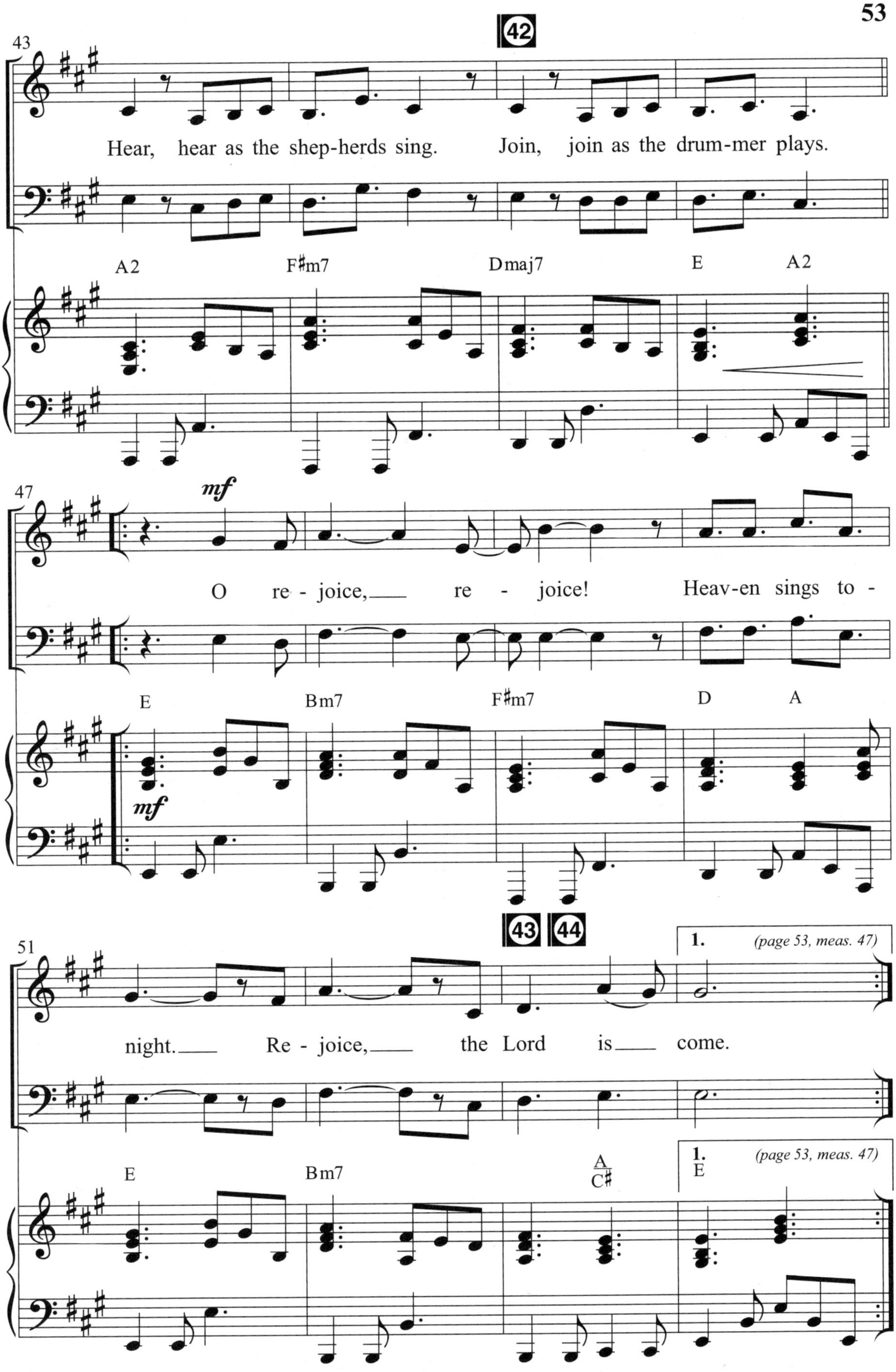
42
43
Hear, hear as the shep-herds sing. Join, join as the drum-mer plays.
A2 F♯m7 Dmaj7 E A2
47
mf
O re - joice, re - joice! Heav-en sings to -
E Bm7 F♯m7 D A
mf
43 44
51
1. (page 53, meas. 47)
night. Re - joice, the Lord is come.
E Bm7 A/C♯ E

King of Heaven

Words and Music by
MATT CROCKER, SALOMON LIGHTHELM
and RYAN TAUBERT
Arranged by Luke Gambill

NARRATOR: Heaven's King came down from His throne, leaving His majesty behind to bring hope to all mankind. *(Music starts)* Born a Child, died a Savior, and now He lives and reigns forevermore! Hallelujah! The King of Heaven, our God with Us, has come!

© Copyright 2013 Hillsong Music Publishing (APRA)
(Administered in the US and Canada at CapitolCMGPublishing.com). All rights reserved. Used by permission.
PLEASE NOTE: Copying of this music is NOT covered by the CCLI license. For CCLI information call 1-800-234-2446.

Holy, Holy, Holy (God with Us)

Lyrics by
REGINALD HEBER

Music by JOHN B. DYKES
New Words and Music by
MATT MAHER
Arranged by Luke Gambill

NARRATOR: Holy, holy, holy is our God Almighty. He who was and is and is to come. *(Music starts)* Let us join together and praise His holy name, for our God, Emmanuel, has come.

© Copyright 2013 Thankyou Music (PRS) (Administered worldwide at CapitolCMGPublishing.com excluding Europe which is administered by Integritymusic.com; songs@integritymusic.com) / Valley of Songs Music (BMI) (Administered at CapitolCMGPublishing.com). All rights reserved. Used by permission.
PLEASE NOTE: Copying of this music is NOT covered by the CCLI license. For CCLI information call 1-800-234-2446.

Gospel of Love
with *Hark! the Herald Angels Sing*

Words and Music by
TRAVIS COTTRELL, DAVID MOFFITT,
SUE C. SMITH and JONATHAN LEE
Arranged by Luke Gambill

NARRATOR: *(Music starts)* Jesus came to give us life, and now we are redeemed. So let us go and preach the Gospel — the Great News to the world — that our God has come to save. This is the Gospel of love!

© Copyright 2012 Universal Music - Brentwood Benson Publishing / Great Revelation Music / CCTB Music (ASCAP) / Universal Music - Brentwood Benson Tunes / Jlee Publishing (SESAC) (Administered at CapitolCMGPublishing.com). All rights reserved. Used by permission.
PLEASE NOTE: Copying of this music is NOT covered by the CCLI license. For CCLI information call 1-800-234-2446.

HARK! THE HERALD ANGELS SING (Charles Wesley, Felix Mendelssohn)